THE PRACTICAL STRATEGIES SERIES
IN GIFTED EDUCATION

series editors
FRANCES A. KARNES & KRISTEN R. STEPHENS

Developing
Mentorship Programs
for Gifted Students

Del Siegle

Routledge
Taylor & Francis Group

NEW YORK AND LONDON

First published 2005 by Prufrock Press Inc.

Published 2021 by Routledge
605 Third Avenue, New York, NY 10017
2 Park Square, Milton Park, Abingdon, Oxon OX14 4RN

Routledge is an imprint of the Taylor & Francis Group, an informa business

ISBN 13: 978-1-59363-172-7 (pbk)

Contents

The Practical Strategies Series in Gifted Education offers teachers, counselors, administrators, parents, and other interested parties up-to-date instructional techniques and information on a variety of issues pertinent to the field of gifted education. Each guide addresses a focused topic and is written by scholars with authority on the issue. Several guides have been published. Among the titles are:

- *Acceleration Strategies for Teaching Gifted Learners*
- *Curriculum Compacting: An Easy Start to Differentiating for High-Potential Students*
- *Enrichment Opportunities for Gifted Learners*
- *Independent Study for Gifted Learners*
- *Motivating Gifted Students*
- *Questioning Strategies for Teaching the Gifted*
- *Social & Emotional Teaching Strategies*
- *Using Media & Technology With Gifted Learners*

For a current listing of available guides within the series, please contact Prufrock Press at (800) 998-2208 or visit http://www.prufrock.com.

What Is Mentoring?

"A single conversation across the table with a wise man
is worth a month's study of books."
                                              —Chinese proverb

Mentoring has existed for as long as one generation has passed
its wisdom to another (Tomlinson, 2001). The basis for the
term originated in Homer's *Odyssey*. Odysseus left his trusted
friend Mentor in charge of his household and his son
Telemachus during his absence. Athena later disguised herself
as Mentor and guided Telemachus in his search for his father
(Pennsylvania State University, 1999–2002).

Mentoring involves a more knowledgeable and experienced individual helping a less experienced individual reach a
major life goal (Goff & Torrance, 1999; Tomlinson, 2001).
This relationship can range from a formal arrangement that is
carefully planned and executed to a serendipitous meeting of
like-minded individuals with a common interest (Nash, 2001;
Tomlinson). The relationship is based on trust and a genuine
desire for growth and learning (Goff & Torrance, 1999).

Mentors are more than role models. In addition to providing skills, they support and challenge as they help their younger charges develop a vision for the future (Kaufmann, 2003). They teach, counsel, engage, and inspire (Nash, 2001) and often serve as friends throughout the process (Silverman, 2000).

Mentorship programs can provide motivated gifted and talented students with an opportunity to apply inductive thinking and problem-solving skills to advanced content that is often associated with real-life situations. Mentorships generally serve one or more of the following student goals:

- career explorations,

- research beyond the scope of the regular classroom,

- opportunity to study topics not available in the regular curriculum,

- development of specific skills, and

- opportunity to work with experts in fields of interest (Idaho, 1999).

Three groups of gifted and talented students particularly benefit from mentorships: highly gifted, disadvantaged, and underachieving students. The highly gifted need challenges well beyond the school's resources; the disadvantaged profit from significant role models, career and college counseling, and possibly summer employment and scholarship opportunities; the underachieving benefit from meaningful learning experiences, individual attention, and a change from the status quo (VanTassel-Baska, 2000)

At the core of mentoring is the practice of mentors' recognizing young people's talents and interests and providing opportunities to explore and develop their skills (Siegle & McCoach, 2005). Mentoring has withstood the test of time because it works under a variety of conditions with individuals of all ages. Mentoring at an early age helps young people recognize and appreciate their own uniqueness (Bennetts, 2001) as they pursue their talents and creativity (Torrance, 1984). Older students benefit even more from mentoring experiences (Roberts & Inman, 2001). Adolescents enjoy working with others apart from their families. They benefit from opportunities for collaboration, assistance with the transition from youth to young adulthood, college and career guidance, chances for choice, and development of their esoteric interests (Bennetts, 2001).

Torrance (1984) documented that mentors make a difference in the educational attainment and creative achievement of their mentees. Students in mentoring relationships have better school attendance, are more likely to attend college, and have better attitudes towards school (Jekielek, Moore, Hair, & Scarupa, 2002). Mentored students stay in school longer and accomplish more as adults (Torrance, 1984). Mentorships increase student self-confidence and self-awareness (Nash, 2001). They promote responsibility and the importance of preparing for the future (Purcell, Renzulli, McCoach, & Spottiswoode, 2001). This includes improved organization and time management skills (Davalos & Haensly, 1997). In addition, when youth enjoy a regular, positive activity with an adult over the course of a year, they are 46% less likely to begin using drugs, 27% less likely to begin using alcohol, and 52% less likely to skip school. (Charityguide, n.d., p. 1)

Gifted students' need for advanced knowledge, inductive learning through exploration and problem solving, and diverse interests make them ideal candidates for mentoring experiences. Gifted and talented students learn more deeply and at an accelerated pace which necessitates assistance beyond conventional classroom and home environments. They need to investigate the complexities and interrelationships among disciplines that can only be discovered with assistance from highly knowledgeable experts. Mentors are also necessary when gifted and talented students have interests that their peers are not prepared to explore (Robert & Inman, 2001). Classroom teachers, gifted and talented specialists, and parents may lack the specialized knowledge necessary to develop gifted students' talents. Mentors provide a level of sophistication and intensity of interest that is normally not accessible from traditional sources (Siegle, 2001). Mentors and mentees form a partnership where they explore their passions and interests (Roberts & Inman, 2001) and unique knowledge and talents (Nash, 2001). The mentee engages in real world learning and has an opportunity to study content in a ceilingless environment beyond the confines of the classroom curriculum (Davalos & Haensly, 1997).

How to Start Developing a Mentoring Program

An ancient Chinese proverb declares that no wind is favorable if one does not know to which port one is sailing. A well-articulated plan that builds broad audience support is essential when starting a mentorship program. Schools, universities, parent groups, service organizations, or businesses usually organize mentoring programs. Regardless of the sponsoring agency, a set of procedures is usually followed in developing a program. For the purpose of this publication, the school will serve as the organizing agency. The first step in planning is to form a planning committee that will be able to

1. Develop a mentoring program specific to the given situation.

2. Build school and community support for the mentoring program.

The committee (Table 1) should include a program coordinator, teachers, a school administrator, a school psychologist or school

Table 1
Planning Committee Member Roles and Functions

Member	Function
Program Coordinator	Organize the committee and direct progress
Teacher	Assess teacher attitudes and build support for the program among the faculty and students
Administrator	Provide insight into program operations, liability issues, budgets, and other resources; build school and community support for the program
Psychologist or Counselor	Contribute guidelines and insight into selecting potential mentors and mentees
Student	Offer a unique perspective on what type of program would be embraced by students to meet their learning needs; build support within the student body.
Parents and Community Members	Assist in building community support and gaining access to potential mentors

counselor, parents, students, and community members (Siegle & McCoach, 2005).

The goals of the committee are to assess the needs of the students, review available resources, and develop a mentoring program matching its purpose with the resources of the school and community.

Mentorships generally serve one or more of three purposes:

- interest and knowledge development,

- career investigations, or

- affective development.

Interest and knowledge development involves expanding the curriculum to enable students with outstanding talent, knowledge, or interest to work with someone with expertise in those areas. The classic mentoring image falls into this category. Career investigation, includes opportunities for students to explore one, or a variety of careers with someone involved in those careers. Finally, affective development involves providing role models who furnish emotional support to increase student self-esteem (Milam, 2001). Each of these purposes meets a different set of student needs. Mentorships can meet all or some of these needs.

Academic tutoring, job shadowing, career exploration, life and job skill development, and participation in internships are common mentorship formats that meet one or a combination of the above three purposes (National Mentoring Partnership, n.d.). Gifted and talented students may have a greater need for some of them. A clear understanding of each option is essential.

Academic Tutoring

Academic tutoring for gifted and talented students differs greatly from academic tutoring for traditional or remedial students. Gifted and talented students need content above and beyond that which is regularly found in the curriculum. Mentoring is necessary when gifted students' talents and interests are "so advanced or divergent from the typical school resources that they need to be placed in situations where those resources are available" (Colemen & Cross, 2001, p. 326). This mentoring is also needed when students' interests are beyond what their peers are ready to explore (Roberts & Inman, 2001). Academic tutor mentoring may include the introduction of topics at an earlier age. It might also include a depth of content not covered in the curriculum at any age. The Study of Mathematically Precocious Youth's (SMPY) Diagnostic Testing–Prescriptive Model is an advanced example of academic tutoring (Lupkowski, Assouline, & Stanley, 1990). In this program, students are exposed to advanced mathematical content at an early age. Academic tutoring can also include opportunities for gifted and talented students to investigate real-world problems as practicing professionals (Renzulli & Reis, 1985). With academic tutoring, the mentor stimulates interest, sets the learning pace, clarifies principles, and extends knowledge based on the student's academic strengths and interests. Academic tutors must possess advanced content knowledge. These mentors should have an academic degree, extensive training, or experience in the discipline (e.g., chemistry) in which they are mentoring students. Rigorous academic credentials are essential for mentors working at the secondary school level because students' expertise in the content is more extensive.

Job Shadowing and Career Exploration

Job shadowing is usually short-term while career exploration covers an extended period of time. During job shadowing, a student may spend a few days to a couple weeks at a mentor's workplace learning about the given career. Job shadowing may evolve into a career exploration where the young person spends an extended amount of in-depth time at the mentor's location. This can occur during a regularly scheduled time each week or during the summer. Students are sometimes paid for these experiences.

Many gifted students have earned sufficient credits for high school graduation. Therefore, they may be able to spend part of each school day exploring career options with a mentor. As mentioned earlier, career exploration is particularly beneficial for gifted and talented students from disadvantaged backgrounds (VanTassel-Baska, 2000). Gifted and talented students who exhibit multi-potentiality are also good candidates for career exploration. These students generally possess a variety of skills and interests. Career exploration may help them focus their interests and talents. Scheduling and transportation are two obstacles that must be overcome for career exploration to work effectively during the school day.

Job Skill Development

Mentors can also assist young people in acquiring career skills that will help them succeed in the workplace and obtain employment. Developing career knowledge is more important for gifted and talented students than developing technical job skills since most gifted and talented students will probably participate in additional educational opportunities beyond high school. Under this option, young people learn skills such as preparing resumes, managing time, and resolving workplace conflicts, many of which can be attained through job shadowing and career exploration. Gifted and talented students, like all students, benefit from the hands-on knowledge gleaned from such experiences.

Internships

Internships are traditionally associated with post secondary education. Most university programs offer internship opportunities for their students. Internships are less common for younger students. High school students may participate in summer internship programs. Such opportunities develop life skills and provide career exploration. Because of their advanced

Student: _____

Mentor Name and Address: _____

_____

Topic: _____

Background

(Name of student) is a senior at Mountain Home High School. He is undertaking this internship under the auspices of the school district's gifted/talented program. Successful completion of this internship will result in one semester elective credit.

Schedule

The internship will begin on (date). The intern will register for the internship for the seventh hour each day and will receive credit based on that registration. Whenever possible the individual work of the internship will be completed during this time. However, sometimes the internship work must be scheduled at other times. The intern may work independently at home during the seventh hour when he is not scheduled for internship work, or he may arrange with the librarian to work in the library at that time. He will meet once a week with the mentor. This meeting will be regularly scheduled for 2:15 at the Pupil Personnel Office. The time and place may occasionally be changed at the discretion of the mentor. A minimum of 70 hours is required to earn this credit. This includes a minimum of one hour weekly contact time with the mentor and the additional time spent on application of skills learned, research, and study.

Make-up Work

If the intern will miss any of his or her regular classes because of this internship, he or she will give a copy of this contract to relevant teachers to explain the situation. The intern should have it cleared ahead of time and make arrangements if he or she is going to miss a class. The principal has indicated that this contract is a waiver of the minimum attendance rule for classes and that no petition will be required to receive credit in the classes missed because of the internship. The intern is responsible for negotiating agreements with his teachers regarding make-up work, tests, etc., so that these absences are not a burden for teachers or disruptive to other students. The intern must give his or her teachers as much advanced notice as possible when he or she will be absent and must turn in make-up work promptly. It is wise to do the make-up work before the day missed, rather than after, whenever possible.

Supervision

During internship activities, the intern will be under the supervision of the mentor and those he or she appoints. However, it is understood that the intern may sometimes be working on his or her own and not in the presence or under the direct supervision of any adult. The mentor will meet with the intern at least once a week and will assign him or her appropriate activities for the times when they cannot meet.

Curriculum

The content of this internship may include but may not be limited to the following: (list of anticipated activities and skills developed)

Transportation

(Name of student) will provide his or her own transportation to the mentor's office or designated work site. During these times, the intern is to travel only to and from the internship and on internship business. The intern is not to transport other people without specific written advanced parental permission. The intern also has permission to ride with his or her mentor, appointee, or facilitator.

Attendance

The school will not keep formal attendance records for the seventh hour. If (name of student) must be absent during any scheduled internship meeting or observation time, he or she should call both the mentor and the high school in advance. If (name of student) is absent from a scheduled meeting or observation time without notification, the mentor will call the high school office.

continued on next page

Figure 1. Sample internship contract

Note. Retrieved October 20, 2004, from http://www.sde.state.id.us/cdpubs/GTmanual.pdf. Reprinted with permission.

continued from previous page

Grading and/or Problems

The intern, his or her parents, and/or the mentor will contact the facilitator if any questions or problems arise. The facilitator will contact them during the internship and at its conclusion for evaluations and feedback. The mentor will evaluate the intern five times including midterms and final grades. The facilitator, as the certified teacher, will have final responsibility for actual grades.

Waiver of Liability

Extending the public school education beyond the school grounds provides increased learning opportunities. It also involves added risks. (Name of student) will be driving during school hours. No security checks are provided by the school system for mentors and other adults with whom the student may work during the internship. There is considerably more student independence and less frequent grading; a student who does not structure work time well and/or who is reluctant to report problems to the facilitator and mentor promptly may risk failing in this course even though he or she typically gets A's in structured courses. (This is unusual; however, most students have great success with these internships.) There may be other risks not stated here. (Name of student) and his or her parents understand that mishaps may occur in the pursuit of this internship. They release the school district, school district personnel and the mentor from liability for mishaps.

Signature Block

Student's Name   _____

Mentor's Name _____

Parent's Name _____

G/T Facilitator _____

School Counselor _____

High School Principal _____

knowledge, gifted and talented students may be ready for internships at an earlier age than their peers. A sample high school internship contract is shown in Figure 1.

The scope of mentoring programs varies in two ways: the extent of total school involvement and the length of the mentoring experience. A program may be organized around a few students with exceptional needs or it may encompass a wider range of students. It may involve students from a single class, or it may extend school-wide. The number of students involved is dependent upon the needs of the student body and the resources of the school. "Schools with a variety of accelerated classes and an extensive honors and Advanced Placement program have different needs than those with a pullout enrichment program or no program at all" (Siegle & McCoach, 2005, p. 486). A school with extensive options for gifted and talented students may simply require mentors for a handful of exceptional students whose academic interests or needs are not being met, while a school with limited opportunities for gifted and talented students may need to involve more students in mentoring relationships. A word of caution is warranted here. A mentoring program should not be used as an easy, or less expensive, solution for meeting the needs of gifted and talented students. Not all gifted and talented students are ready for, or would benefit from, mentoring. Mentoring is only one of several options that schools should offer gifted and talented students.

In addition to the breath of services, the length of the mentorship is also important. Longer mentoring relationships are usually better. Youth in short-term mentoring relationships (3 to 6 months) do not show significant improvement, and students involved in briefer mentoring relationships often report being less confident about doing their schoolwork and have lower self-worth. Mentoring requires a sustained relationship over time. The frequency of contact is also important. Students in mentorships with frequent mentor contact have higher grades, greater confidence about schoolwork, fewer school absences, and are more likely to attend college than students who occasionally meet with their mentors (Jekielek et al., 2002). Therefore, while schools may wish to limit the number of students who participate in a mentoring program, they should provide a sustained mentoring experience over time for those students who are involved. The interactions can range from assistance with long-term projects to simple tasks such as providing students with feedback on their schoolwork.

In addition to assessing the students' needs, the school's resources must also be evaluated. This includes reviewing staff competencies, administrative support and space availability, and program funding. New staff may need to be hired to manage the program. This may include hiring a program coordinator and clerical assistant. If current staff is available, funds may be needed to train them. If mentoring occurs on campus, mentors and mentees need space and possibly additional equipment for their meetings. If the meetings occur off campus, space is still needed for program records and administrative support. Some programs provide mentors with a stipend or financial support for travel and materials. Even programs with volunteer mentors require funds for promotion, training, daily operations, and program evaluation. The school's liability insurance must be reviewed to accommodate the unique legal issues associated with the mentoring program.

The format and goals of the mentorship program can vary. The most common format is a person-to-person commitment. More recently, and one of the fastest growing formats, is telementoring, also known as virtual mentoring, e-mentoring (Nash, 2001), or iMentoring (Buery, n.d.). Students involved in telementoring often develop class projects using e-mail or the World Wide Web. These usually include a three-component design involving a student, his or her teacher, and a mentor. For example, a student, with assistance from his or her teacher, will propose a mentoring project. They will propose the project to an organization such as the International Telementor Program (ITP), which will assist in locating a mentor.

Telementoring is popular because it allows mentors to use their time effectively and efficiently. Communication usually occurs through e-mail or online discussion forums to ensure privacy and security. These communications are frequently monitored to safeguard the mentee and limit liability to the mentor and the sponsoring organization. Some of the advantages of telementoring are

- connecting thousands of professionals with students on a scale that is impractical in traditional face-to-face mentoring;

- matching students with appropriate mentors without geographic limitations;

- allowing convenient, consistent, weekly communication between students and mentors without travel;

- creating an archive of all communication for monitoring and evaluation purposes;

- eliminating scheduling problems between mentors and students because an e-mail communication can be sent any time from a variety of locations; and

- providing the opportunity for students to work on long-term projects with their mentors (ITP, n.d.).

Telementoring becomes even more important for students with obscure interests from rural and low-income communities. Educators and parents in low-income communities or rural areas may find it difficult to locate a nearby mentor for a student with an atypical interest.

Telementoring need not be limited to participation with a national program. Classroom teachers or gifted and talented coordinators can match their students with adults through e-mail pen pals in their community. Initially it is more convenient to locate community people who are willing to serve as electronic resources; however, the participant pool can expand to include contacts around the country or even the world. If the mentor pool is in the area, a kickoff event such as a pizza party for the participating students and mentors can help acquaint the pairs.

Face-to-face mentoring is more common. This usually involves one mentor working with one student, although groups of mentors sometimes collaborate with groups of students. One-on-one mentorships tend to build strong relationships, while group mentoring can provide the necessary flexibility many busy mentors require. The remainder of this publication focuses on face-to-face mentoring.

How Are Mentors and Mentees Selected?

Not all gifted and talented students require mentors, nor are all gifted and talented students good candidates for mentorships. Highly motivated students with focused interests are the best candidates for mentoring. These students usually have independent work habits, a strong grasp of subject matter, and a desire to be mentored (Roberts & Inman, 2001). They are goal driven and can articulate a clear purpose for their mentorship.

Students who are disenfranchised with their educational program sometime indicate that they wish to work on their own with a mentor. The fact that students indicate they wish to work on their own does not necessarily mean a mentorship is the best arrangement. Reilly (1992) notes that "on my own" can depict a desire to study a topic of interest not covered in the curriculum, to move more or less rapidly through the curriculum, to work individually instead of in a group, to produce a different product than was assigned, or to see connections between the content and the "real world." She cautions that schools have the primary responsibility to educate children; therefore, educators should investigate a variety of available resources within the school before asking others for a mentoring commitment.

Figure 2 shows a rating scale that can be used to evaluate students' potential for mentorships. The scale is used to rate students' readiness for a mentorship in five areas: advanced knowledge and skills, creative initiative, persistence, responsibility, and interpersonal relations. Students who are successful mentees demonstrate strengths in these areas (Minority Engineering and Computer Science Program, n.d.; Nash & Treffinger, 1993). Students who are selected for mentorships must be willing to invest significant amounts of time with their mentors. Young children may spend an hour per week with a mentor while high school students generally spend several hours each week with their mentors. Students with the characteristics listed on the Mentee Selection Scale are more likely to invest the time and energy necessary for a successful mentoring experience.

Students with a passing interest in a topic or an idle curiosity are not good candidates for mentorships. Effective mentorships require a sustained relationship over time. An authentic mentorship for gifted and talented students should include real-world applications of the student's passion or interest. They also should include opportunities for increased knowledge and expansion of the student's gifts (Roberts & Inman, 2001). Rimm (2003) recommended that potential mentees reflect on the following questions before entering into a mentoring relationship:

- What do I hope to get from this relationship?

- What type of adult would I get along with best?

- Are there any special skills or interests that I want my mentor to have?

- What can I do to help my mentor bring out the best in me?

- How can I help my mentor in return? (p. 91)

As related to the potential mentoring topic, the student . . .

	Never	Rarely	Occasionally	Frequently	Always
1. is not being challenged by traditional educational methods and activities	☐	☐	☐	☐	☐
2. possesses extensive vocabulary on the topic	☐	☐	☐	☐	☐
3. asks questions that are not being answered by classes or the present curriculum	☐	☐	☐	☐	☐
4. shows evidence of previous and current active involvement with the topic	☐	☐	☐	☐	☐
5. focuses and exerts extended effort on tasks related to the topic	☐	☐	☐	☐	☐
6. maintains curiosity and interest in the topic	☐	☐	☐	☐	☐
7. displays a personal sense of responsibility and autonomy.	☐	☐	☐	☐	☐
8. knows or is willing to learn process or methodology skills related to the topic	☐	☐	☐	☐	☐
9. is open to guidance and suggestions	☐	☐	☐	☐	☐
10. easily interacts with adults	☐	☐	☐	☐	☐
Add Column Total:	☐	☐	☐	☐	☐
Multiply by Weight:	x 1	x 2	x 3	x 4	x 5
Add Weighted Column Totals:	☐ +	☐ +	☐ +	☐ +	☐

Scale Total: _____ / 50

Figure 2. Mentee Selection Scale for evaluating students who are likely candidates for mentorship experiences

Potential mentees can also provide valuable information about themselves when they apply for a mentorship. A mentee application should include information about the student's interests, talents, and expectations as they relate to the mentorship. Figure 3 depicts a possible mentee application form that collects data in these areas. Prior to accepting a student for a mentorship, the selection committee should review the students' past academic accomplishments and record of school participation. Such information can be gleaned from students' school records as well as current and previous teachers. School attendance, academic grades, extra curricular participation, personal responsibility, and attitudes toward school are areas where data should be reviewed. Students' parents and peers can also be consulted. They may provide additional insight about potential mentees that is not available from other sources.

Torrance (1984) noted that in order to sustain a mentorship "it seems certain that both persons in a mentorship must continue to grow and contribute to each other's growth" (p. 19). Mentors must be secure and confident in their own skills and be aware and able to control their own jealousy, competitiveness, and frustration tolerance. One researcher described one of her mentors as "quick to praise, slow to criticize, and confident enough in his own ability to share the limelight with others" (Lashaway-Bokina, 1996, p. v). Mentors must be able to creatively teach inductively and at higher levels. In addition to all of this, they must motivate (Shaughnessy & Neely, 1991). "Mentors do not so much teach as live the process . . . and in so doing provide for others a foundation for learning and living throughout the lifespan" (Bennetts, 2001, p. 260).

Potential mentors must not only be caring and generous with their time, they must also understand and appreciate their mentee's giftedness. Mentors who are gifted themselves may facilitate this. A good mentor is described as a "guide on the side, not a sage on the stage." This particularly applies to mentors working with gifted and talented students. Mentors must also respect their mentees' right to make their own choices.

They must be open to different ideas and different points of view. They need to be able to provide constructive, rather than critical, feedback. Finally, while it seems obvious, they must be comfortable being a role model and having the responsibility that entails (Siegle & McCoach, 2005). Berger (1990) added that mentors must like working with gifted and talented students, have a teaching style that is compatible with their mentee's learning style, share an excitement and joy of learning, and be optimistic about the future. In other words, skill in an area is not sufficient for mentoring, a mentor must have the desire and ability to develop a nurturing relationship (Roberts & Inman, 2001).

Potential mentors are everywhere. The local car mechanic may have a master's degree in sociology and the kindly woman down the street may have served as a foreign correspondent. Seniors citizens are excellent resources. They often have the talent, experiences, and time necessary to be successful mentors. It is important to look beyond individuals' current occupations. For example, many teachers have worked in other professions before earning their teaching certificates. These educators can bring a myriad of real-world experience to a mentorship. Mentors can be found in

- area colleges and universities (professors as well as students),

- K–12 schools,

- service groups and community organizations,

- research institutes,

- cultural institutes (art, science, music, etc.),

- government agencies,

Name:_____

Date: _____ Age: _____

Parent(s)/guardian name(s): _____

Address:_____

Home phone: (___) _____

Emergency contact: _____ phone: (___) _____

Student e-mail:_____

Parent/guardian e-mail:_____

Race/Ethnicity/Nationality: (Please check all that apply)

___ Asian   ___ Black/African American

___ Caucasian   ___ Native American/American Indian

___ Hispanic/Latin America   ___ Other _____

Help us get to know you by answering the following questions.

My interests and talents:
- In what extra curricular, outside, or after school activities have you been involved?
- In what area/topic are you seeking a mentor?
- How long have you been interested in this topic?
- How did you first know you were interested in this topic?
- What outside activities or resources have you used to learn more about this topic?
- What are some unanswered questions you have about this topic?
- What is special about you that you will bring to the mentorship?

What I expect:
- Why do you think you would be successful in a mentorship?
- How can a mentor help you?
- What do you hope to gain from a mentorship?
- One year from now, what would you like to say you accomplished as a result of your mentorship?

About my mentor:
- What type of adult would make the best mentor for you?
- What special interests and skills should your mentor possess?
- How much time do you think you can spend with your mentor each week?

Other skills and talents:
Please rate your skills in the following areas by checking the appropriate column:

	I do this well	I am average at this	I could be better at this
Time management	O	O	O
Study skills	O	O	O
Social skills	O	O	O
Interpersonal skills	O	O	O
Self-advocacy	O	O	O
Assertiveness	O	O	O
Goal setting	O	O	O
Stress management	O	O	O
Problem solving	O	O	O
Library research skills	O	O	O
Internet research skills	O	O	O
Technology skills	O	O	O

Of the above areas, specifically describe your skills in the one area in which you are best.

Yes, I want to be a part of (name of mentoring program). Please consider my application to be a mentee in the (program name).

_____   _____
Student signature   Date

I support _____ (student's name) and would like her/him to participate in the (name of mentoring program) for the 2005–2006 school year.

_____   _____
Parent/legal guardian signature   Date

Figure 3. Possible mentee application that can be used to collect information about potential mentee's interests, talents, and expectations as they relate to the mentorship

Note. Retrieved October 20, 2004, from http://www.sde.state.id.us/cdpubs/GTmanual.pdf. Copyright © Idaho Department of Education. Reprinted with permission.

- media (television, radio, newspaper, advertising, publishing),

- local businesses,

- libraries,

- sports organizations,

- outdoor and environmental organizations,

- professions (medicine, law, education, engineering, literature, architecture, art), and

- senior citizen centers (Nash & Treffinger, 1993).

The Community Talent Miner (Figure 4) was developed by Reva Friedman-Nimz and Emily Stewart (Renzulli, 1977) to locate community members who can work with young people. While it is dated, it is still a useful instrument for locating potential mentors. Copies of the Community Talent Miner can be disseminated to various organizations and groups within the community. For example, copies of the Community Talent Miner could be shared with the leader of the local Kiwanis who could distribute and collect them at a monthly meeting. After reviewing the completed Talent Miners, the mentorship program director might contact potential mentors and discuss various options for being involved in the mentorship program. Distributing the Community Talent Miner through personal contact is much more effective than simply leaving them at a location. The Community Talent Miner works well because it helps potential mentors reflect on their skills and experiences.

The program director and members of the mentorship committee, if one exists, must be vigilant talent scouts. This includes contacting personal and business associates who might serve as mentors and scanning the local newspaper for articles and stories about interesting community members who could serve as mentors. The National Mentoring Center (n.d.) created a catchy postcard that can be sent to potential mentors. The message simply reads, "You have received this postcard because somebody believes you would make a great mentor."

Many small programs prefer to begin by involving a group of mentors at a single business rather that a group of mentors from various locations. As one organizer noted, "I didn't want to get a geographic spread of people. I wanted them to all be in one location because I felt, as important as it was to have mentors, it was just as important to train the mentors" (Robb, 1997, p. 11).

Mentors must provide sufficient background information to evaluate their potential as a mentor. This should include

- pertinent training and experience related to the topic they are mentoring,

- previous mentoring experiences,

- previous experience working with young people,

- reasons for wishing to mentor a young person, and

- references who can attest to the potential mentor's expertise and personal character.

A sample mentor application form is shown in Figure 5.

Name: _____ Date: _____

Address: _____

Telephone: _____

E-mail: _____ Fax: _____

Place of Business: _____

In filling out this questionnaire, please keep in mind:
1. There are no predetermined responses. Be as original as you like in your replies.
2. Take as much space as you need to respond to any item. Use the back of the sheet if necessary.
3. If there are sections or questions you'd rather omit, simply skip them.

I. Trips, Safaris, and Excursions

1. Have you traveled "off the beaten track"—to any unusual or out-of-the-way places?
2. Where did you go (include dates)?
3. What sorts of records do you have of your travels (e.g., photographs, local products, or other artifacts)?

II. Academic Experience

1. If you attended college, business school, or had technical training, what subject was your major emphasis?
2. Did it have any unusual aspects (e.g., an interdisciplinary major, involvement in original research, publications, or presentations)? Please list.

III. Intercultural Experiences

1. Have you lived in another culture? If so, where?
2. For how long and under what circumstances did you live in the culture?
3. Describe one meaningful experience you had during your visit.

IV. Hobbies, Collections, and Competitions

1. What are your hobbies?
2. Are you a collector? If so, what sorts of things do you collect?
3. How did you become involved with your hobby or collection?
4. Do you belong to an organized group of people with like interests (e.g., Stamp Collectors of America, Flat Earth Society)? Please list.
5. Have you entered your collection or hobby in a competition (include details and outcomes)?
6. Have you ever entered any other unusual competitions or contests (e.g., a frog jumping contest, limerick competition, model sailboat race)? What sort? Is this something in which you participate on a regular basis?

V. Esoteric Topical Interests

Most of us know people who describe themselves as history buffs, computer whizzes, ecology nuts, science fiction freaks, committed health food faddists, or hopeless Sherlock Holmes addicts. Could you think of a special interest of yours for which you'd give yourself a similar label? Please include area of interest and labels.

1.   In what ways have you followed up on your interests?
2.   Do you meet with other people who have similar interests (include group names, any organized activities, etc.)?

VI. Community-Related Activities

Directions: For each item, include group name(s), positions held, dates of involvement, and how you became involved.

Have you ever:
1.   Lobbied for something?
2.   Belonged to an interest group?
3.   Campaigned for a cause or a person?
4.   Been involved in a religious group?
5.   Joined a community action group?
6.   Donated time to a "charitable" organization?

VII. Professional Experiences

1.   What do you do for a living?
2.   How long has it been your career?
3.   What other career(s) have you explored? How?
4.   How did you select your current career?
5.   How long have you worked at your present job? Please provide a short description of your position.
6.   Which unique or creative aspects of your profession would you like to communicate to a young person who might be interested in entering your field (e.g., skills you have had to learn "the hard way")?

Of those areas explored in this questionnaire, the following are ones about which I am especially enthusiastic:

I would be willing for the teacher(s) of _____ to contact me regarding possible applications of some of my interests and talents with students.

_____

(Your Signature)

Figure 4. The Community Talent Miner: A survey for locating community resources

Note. From *The Enrichment Triad Model: A Guide for Developing Defensible Programs for the Gifted and Talented*, by J. S. Renzulli (pp. 84–86), Mansfield Center, CT: Creative Learning Press. Copyright ©1977 by Creative Learning Press. Reprinted with permission.

University
YWCA
YOUTH MENTOR PROGRAM
2600 Bancroft Way, Berkeley, CA 94704
(510) 848-6370; ywcaymp@earthlink.net

Mentor Application

Name: _____ Gender: M / F Date: _____

Local Address: _____

_____

Permanent Address: _____

_____

Local Phone #: _____ Permanent #: _____

Mobile Phone #: _____ Other #: _____

E-mail Address: _____ Do you check your e-mail? Y / N

Other E-mail Addresses: _____

Date of Birth: _____ Ethnicity: _____

Do You Speak Any Languages Other Than English? _____

Current Class Level: _____ Expected Graduation Date: _____

Major/Minor: _____

Will you be employed during the current academic year? If so, please note how many hours and days.

What other programs, clubs, or activities will you be involved in during the current year? How much time do you expect to commit to them?

Will you be able to commit three hours a week to meet your mentee and participate in group activities for the rest of the academic year? Y / N

Do you have a car? Y / N   Would you like to carpool with other mentors? Y / N

How did you learn of the Youth Mentor Program?

What interested you most about being a mentor for the Youth Mentor Program? Why do you want to be a mentor?

What skills would you contribute to the program? How will they enhance your ability to be a youth mentor?

Please describe any prior experience you have had working with youth and why it would prepare you to be an effective and positive mentor.

What are your interests and how do you enjoy spending your time?

Please describe any additional information that would be helpful in the selection and matching process.

To complete your application we require 2 references, one from a current /previous employer, instructor, or other professional who can validate your skills and abilities; and one from a person who has known you for at least two years (not a relative). Please list below the name, relationship to you, phone number, and email address of each person from whom you are using as a reference.

1. Name _____
    Relationship _____
    Phone _____ E-mail _____

2. Name _____
    Relationship _____
    Phone _____ E-mail _____

Have you ever been convicted of a criminal act? Y / N
If yes please explain:

Your Signature: _____ Date: _____

Figure 5. Sample mentor application

Note. Retrieved June 8, 2004, from http://www.ywca-berkeley.org/mentor.html. Copyright ©2004 YWCA at U.C. Berkeley. Reprinted with permission.

How Can We Assure Successful Mentorships?

Liability

The safety and well being of students is the number one priority of any mentoring program. Many schools conduct criminal checks on mentor volunteers (Roberts & Inman, 2001). Some programs require parents to accompany their children during mentoring times. All of the mentors should be known or recommended by a reliable source (Forster, 1994). The National Mentoring Partnership (n.d.) recommends the following steps to minimize liability and increase student safety.

- *Screen volunteers before signing them on as mentors.* Potential volunteers should be willing to undergo an application process similar to standard hiring policies: an interview, reference check with at least three people, and a check of their work history. If the mentors will be working one-on-one with youth, fingerprints and a police record check should be conducted.

- *Develop a "Mentor's Code of Conduct" that spells out the program's policies.* The code should cover appropriate activities for mentors and mentees, explicit rules regarding alcohol and drugs, and boundaries of mentor/participant relationships. The code also must advise mentors and staff of the absolute need to respect mentees' confidentiality. A sample code of conduct is shown in Figure 6.

- *Maintain ongoing contact with volunteers.* Provide training and individual support to help prevent problems in the mentor relationship or solve them before they become crises.

- *Make safety issues a part of mentor training.* Talk about dealing with fire emergencies, using potentially hazardous office equipment, transporting tools, and working in unfamiliar neighborhoods.

- *Require mentors, mentees and their parents to sign release forms.* Before committing to being mentors, volunteers need to know exactly what their obligations are and the extent to which they are protected by the organization's insurance.

- *Consult with legal counsel.* Design a strong risk management plan.

Because student safety is the first priority, mentorship coordinators must extensively screen mentors and vigilantly monitor mentoring relationships once they begin. Other liability issues must also be addressed. The Nebraska Work-Based Project (Nebraska Department of Education, 1998) suggests the following insurance considerations for parents, school administrators, and employees.

The purpose of this Code of Conduct is to ensure the safety and well-being of all participants. Mentors will:

- Represent themselves with dignity and pride and present a positive role model for youth.

- Conduct themselves in a courteous and respectful manner.

- Not consume alcohol or illegal drugs before or during work with young people.

- Not smoke at any time in the Count Basie Learning Center building or grounds.

- Comply with equal opportunity and anti-discrimination laws.

- Work with young people only at the designated places: supervised rooms at the Count Basie Learning Center facility.

- Not take their mentees on outings without prior arrangement with CBLC staff and written permission from parents or legal guardians. (Note that it is not advisable to transport children in your private automobile).

- Accept no monetary compensation for services provided.

It is important that all volunteers comply with the Code of Conduct. Failure to do so may lead to dismissal from the Tutor/Mentoring program.

I will notify the CBLC office at least two weeks in advance if I am unable to continue mentoring. I agree to comply with this Code of Conduct. I authorize the Count Basie Learning Center to make and use photo and video images of me for educational and promotional purposes.

Mentor: _____ Date: _____

CBLC Staff: _____ Date: _____

Figure 6. Sample mentor code of ethics

- *Automobile accident insurance*—provided by the student/ parent (for travel to and from activities) unless the district provides transportation.

- *Accident/liability insurance*—the employer, school district, and family should carry insurance for personal injury or property damage; additional liability (malpractice) insurance may be advisable in the health care field.

- *Worker's compensation*—students participating in paid, work site experiences are covered by worker's compensation and may be covered by the school district's policy or the employer. Students participating in unpaid work site experiences are not covered by worker's compensation; but, if they are injured at the work site, the school district or business's liability insurance, their family insurance, or both may cover them.

- *Medical treatment waiver*—parents sign a waiver for student's participation in a work site learning experience.

Matching Mentors and Mentees

Selecting the right mentor can be a difficult task and several factors must be taken into consideration when matching mentors and mentees. First, the mentee must identify with the mentor.

According to Rimm (2001), identification with a role model is based on three factors. First, mentees must view their mentors as *nurturing and warm*. Encouragement is particularly important to females (Torrance, 1984). Second, mentees must see themselves as *similar* to their mentors. This could include common interests, similar physical characteristics, or comparable backgrounds. For example, female mentees tend to prefer women mentors, while male mentees tend to prefer male mentors. Unfortunately, Shaughnessy and Neely (1991) found a shortage of mentors for females because females who have worked their way up male-dominated field are reluctant to serve as mentors, while social pressure and concern about appearances discourage older men from mentoring younger women. Race by itself does not appear to play a significant role in determining whether mentors and mentees form a strong relationship. Any effects of race appear to be mediated by gender and the mentor's interpersonal style (Jucovy, 2002). Despite these findings, many researchers still believe efforts should be made to match students with mentors who share their ethnic background (Career Academy Support Network, n.d.). Third, the mentee must view the mentor as having some *power*. The mentor must appear to have some authority and autonomy. In other words, the mentor must demonstrate some control and direction over his or her situation.

Kaufmann (2003) suggested that mentors ought to be at least 15 years older than their mentees. She felt this limited competition between them since the mentors would already be established in their careers. The age span also enabled the mentor to guide from a perspective of experience.

The mentor's teaching style should be compatible with the mentee's learning style (Berger, 1990; Kaufmann, 2003). This includes the amount of structure each requires, learning modalities (e.g., auditory, visual, or kinesthetic), instructional style (e.g., reading, discussing), and learning style (e.g., time of day, mobility). Table 2 depicts some common style inventories. Mentors and mentees should share similar values and attitudes.

Mentors and mentees should have an opportunity to express a preference regarding a match, understand how matching decisions are made, and be given an opportunity to request a different match if their original match is not satisfactory after reasonable effort. (Siegle & McCoach, 2005, p. 502)

Table 2
Common Learning and Thinking Style Inventories

Instrument	Preference Assessed
My Way: An Expression Style Inventory (Kettle, Renzulli, & Rizza,1998)	Mode of expression (e.g., drama, written)
Learning Style Inventory (Renzulli, Rizza, & Smith, 2002)	Method of instruction (e.g., peer teaching, projects)
Learning Style Inventory (Dunn, Dunn, & Price, 2000)	23 learning styles (e.g., motivation, visual-auditory-tactile)
Thinking Styles Questionnaire (Sternberg, 1994)	Sternberg's Mental Self-Government Model (e.g., judicial)
Gregorc Style Delineator (Gregorc, 1985)	Gregorc's Mind Styles (e.g., concrete sequential)
Myers-Briggs Type Indicator (Briggs & Myers, 1977)	Jung-Myers-Briggs typological approach to personality

Note. From "Extending Learning Through Mentorships" (p. 498) by D. Siegle & D. B. McCoach (2005) in F. A. Karnes & S. M. Bean (Eds.), *Methods and Materials for Teaching the Gifted* (2nd ed., pp. 473–518). Waco, TX: Prufrock Press. Copyright ©2005 by Prufrock Press. Reprinted with permission.

Training

Seven out of 10 mentors dropout within the first 3 months of mentoring when there isn't adequate training and screening. All mentors and mentees should participate in an orientation experience. These can include separate as well as combined orientations. The orientations should include an overview of the program, a discussion of what is expected of mentors and mentees, and an explanation of the mentors' and mentees' rights.

The orientation meetings should cover the four, growth stages that mentorships traditionally follow. Initially, mentors and mentees learn about each other as they identify their common interests and goals. Neither party has developed trust at this stage, and communication is awkward. Typically this stage lasts from one to six meetings. Mentors and mentees begin confiding in each other during stage two. This stage usually lasts 1 to 3 months, during which they establish attainable expectations for the mentorship. During the third stage goals begin to be accomplished, some goals are modified, and new goals are set. Finally, closure begins, and the mentoring relationship may be redefined (Letting Education Achieve Dreams, n.d.).

A mentor training session typically lasts about 2 hours. During that time the following topics are often discussed:

- steps in the formal mentoring process (see preceding paragraph),

- how to assist mentees in developing goals and planning activities,

- key mentor and mentee process skills (active listening, building trust, ways to be encouraging, opening doors of communication, managing risks, providing corrective feedback, showing initiative, managing the relationship, scheduling meetings, and career awareness),

- how to conduct a basic evaluation of the mentee's progress and the mentorship relationship,

- how often and when to communicate the mentee's progress to the school and parents,

- unexpected challenges and solutions (including termination procedures if they become necessary),

- appropriate and inappropriate behavior,

- maintaining confidentiality, and

- understanding of diversity and cultural awareness.

Evaluation

Evaluation is an essential component of every mentorship program. Two aspects of a program warrant evaluation: satisfaction with the individual mentorships and effectiveness of the overall program operations.

Three initial concerns over the individual mentorships that warrant early evaluation are the effectiveness of the match, the mentor's willingness to recognize and develop the mentee's talent, and the mentee's satisfaction with the mentorship experience (Siegle & McCoach, 2005). An evaluation can be as simple as asking mentors and mentees about their experiences. Evaluations can also be included as part of follow-up activities in which students write or discuss their experiences. Following are some sample evaluation questions for the mentee.

1. In what ways has this mentorship met your expectations? In what ways has it not met them?

2. What problems have you had with the mentorship? How did you work them out?

3. Are you currently having any problems? What are your ideas for working on them?

4. What things have you actually done so far?

5. What would you like to do that you have not been able to do so far?

6. How does this mentorship fit into your long-range goals?

7. How does this mentorship compare to your other school experiences?

8. Would you recommend to a close friend that he or she participate in a mentorship?

9. What has been your favorite thing about the mentorship? Your least favorite?

10. What else would you like to tell me? (Idaho, 1999)

More formal evaluations cover the processes and the outcomes of the program. Process information pertains to the number of mentor/mentee matches, types of activities that were held, length of the mentorship relations, frequency and duration of meetings, and perceptions of the relationship. Outcome information might include data such as the mentee's grades, behaviors, and attitudes; the teacher's reports of the mentee's classroom conduct; the mentor's reflections on his or her experiences; the mentee's optimism about the future; parent-child relationships; and graduation rates (National Mentoring Partnership, n.d.). The mentor's feedback regarding the mentee's progress is also important. A sample form for a mentor's evaluating of a mentorship is shown in Figure 7.

"If the program goals were clearly articulated at the start of the program, evaluating them is an easy task. Without clearly defined goals, deciding how to define program success can be difficult" (Siegle & McCoach, 2005, p. 507).

Mentor's Name _____

Student's Name _____

Mentorship Topic _____ Date _____

Please evaluate the mentorship by circling the appropriate number on the rating scale. If an item is not applicable to this situation, write "NA" to the left of the number. You may write comments on the back of this form to clarify or amplify the evaluation.

	Poor	Average	Good	Excellent
1. Attendance and promptness	1	2	3	4
2. Courtesy	1	2	3	4
3. Appropriate appearance	1	2	3	4
4. Attentiveness	1	2	3	4
5. Responsibility	1	2	3	4
6. Prementorship skills and background	1	2	3	4
7. Growth of understanding of topic	1	2	3	4
8. Meets deadline	1	2	3	4
9. Benefits from critique	1	2	3	4
10. Quantity of work	1	2	3	4
11. Effective use of time	1	2	3	4
12. Works independently	1	2	3	4
13. Quality of work content	1	2	3	4
14. Quality of work presentation	1	2	3	4
15. Takes initiative	1	2	3	4

Recommended Grade:

Comments:

_____   _____

Mentor's signature   Date

Figure 7. Sample mentor's evaluation of a mentorship.

Note. Adapted from the Mountain Home High School Intern Interview by Rita Hoffman. Retrieved October 20, 2004, from http://www.sde.state.id.us/cdpubs/GTmanual.pdf. Copyright © Idaho Department of Education. Reprinted with permission.

Final Remarks

"Often the gifted do not fail intellectually, but emotionally. Obstacles or circumstances become so overwhelming that even the best consider giving up."
—McGreevy (1990, p. 8)

Each year hundreds of thousands of young people benefit from the wisdom and dedication of adult mentors. Some of those relationships occur naturally, others are carefully planned. Some are part of a district-wide mentoring program, others are simple arrangements made by a classroom teacher. What all of them have in common is a meaningful interaction that occurs when individuals with common interests connect. Gifted and talented students can benefit greatly from the mentoring process.

Like any educational service, developing a mentorship requires careful planning. A number of questions must be addressed before starting a program.

- What should the scope of the program be?

- Who will coordinate the program?

- What funding is needed? How will it be obtained?

- What policies need to be developed?

- What liability issues need to be addressed?

- How will mentors be recruited and screened?

- Will mentors be reimbursed?

- How will mentees be selected?

- How will mentors and mentees be matched?

- Where and when will the mentoring take place? What about transportation?

- What should be included in parent, student, and mentor orientations?

- What support will be needed for retention?

- Under what circumstances will mentorships be terminated?

- How much communication is necessary among mentors, mentees, parents, and the program?

- How will individual mentorships and the overall program be evaluated?

The answers to these questions vary from one school to another. Assistance in answering them can be found within the text and resources provided in this publication. Mentoring is one of the most powerful tools schools can develop for cultivating young people's gifts and talents. As Tomlinson (2001) noted, "The idea of mentoring is old. At its core, a mentorship reflects the way in which humans have always passed on their legacy, their artistry" (p. 5).

Resources

Suggestions for Further Reading

Nash, D., & Treffinger, D. (1993). *The mentor kit: A step-by-step guide to creating an effective mentor program in your school.* Waco, TX: Prufrock Press.

Reilly, J. (1992). *Mentorships: The essential guide for schools and business.* Dayton: Ohio Psychology Press.

Siegle, D., & McCoach, D. B. (2005). Extending learning through mentorships. In F. A. Karnes & S. M. Bean (Eds.), *Methods and materials for teaching the gifted* (2nd ed., pp. 473–518). Waco, TX: Prufrock Press.

Torrance, E. P. (1984). *Mentor relationships: How they aid creative achievement, endure, change, and die.* Buffalo, NY: Bearly Limited.

Torrance, E. P., Goff, K., & Satterfield, N. B. (1998). *Multicultural mentoring of the gifted and talented.* Waco, TX: Prufrock Press.

Suggested Web Sites

Career Academy Support Network
http://casn.berkeley.edu/resources/mentor_handbook.html

> Contains a 59-page handbook for developing and managing career academies mentorships. The handbook contains training activities and a variety of management forms.

International Telementor Program
http://www.telementor.org

> Students and potential mentors can register at this site for telementoring experiences. The site also includes valuable information on the telementor process.

Letting Education Achieve Dreams
http://www.uhv.edu/lead/mentoring.htm

> Contains background information on mentoring, information about mentor ethics, and a list of frequently asked questions.

MadSci Network
http://www.madsci.org

> Students can post questions related to science that are answered by a pool of scientists.

Mentoring Partnership of Minnesota
http://www.mentoringworks.org

> While this site offers information about their organization, much of the information can be applied to local mentorship programs.

National Mentoring Partnership
http://www.mentoring.org

> This is one of the most extensive mentorship related sites on the Internet. Contains step-by-step instructions for developing and running a mentoring program. Also provides links to established mentoring programs.

Nebraska State Department of Education's Work-Based Learning Project
http://www.nde.state.ne.us/TECHPREP/WBL/

> Useful forms for beginning mentoring programs are found here.

Northwest Regional Lab's National Mentoring Center
http://www.nwrel.org/mentoring

> Publications and Web resources on mentoring are available at this site.

Pitsco's Ask an Expert
http://www.askanexpert.com

> This is a student-friendly site that features hundreds of experts who field students' questions.

The Mentoring Center
http://www.mentor.org

> Developed by a tax-exempt, private, nonprofit organization in the San Francisco Bay area, this site contains information on mentoring and links to mentoring programs.

References

Bennetts, C. (2001). Fanning the aesthetic flame: Learning for life. *Gifted Education International, 15*, 252–261.

Berger, S. L. (1990). *Mentor relationships and gifted learners* (Digest #E486). (ERIC Document Reproduction Service No. ED321491)

Briggs, K. C., & Myers, I. B. (1977). *Myers-Briggs Type Indicator form G.* Palo Alto, CA: Consulting Psychologists Press.

Buery, R. (n.d.). *Building electronic bridges to connect mentors and young people.* Retrieved March 15, 2003, from http://www.uwnyc.org/technews/v3_n6_a2.html

Career Academy Support Network. (n.d.). *Mentoring handbook for career academies.* Retrieved November 15, 2004, from http://casn.berkeley.edu/resources/mentor_handbook.html

Charityguide (n.d.). *How to make a difference in a few hours: Mentor at-risk kids.* Retrieved November 20, 2004, from http://charityguide.org/charity/fewhours/mentor.htm

Coleman, L. J., & Cross, T. L. (2001). *Being gifted in school: An introduction to development, guidance, and teaching.* Waco, TX: Prufrock Press.

Davalos, R. A., & Haensly, P. A. (1997). After the dust has settled: Youth reflect on their high school mentored research experience. *Roeper Review, 19*, 204–207.

Dunn, R., Dunn, K., & Price, G. (2000). *Learning style inventory*. Lawrence, KS: Price Systems.

Forster, J. (1994). Mentor links program. *Gifted Education International, 10*, 24–30.

Goff, K., & Torrance, E. P. (1999). Discovering and developing giftedness through mentoring. *Gifted Child Today, 22*(3), 14–15, 52–53.

Gregorc, A. F. (1985). *Gregorc style delineator: A self-assessment instrument for adults*. Columbia, CT: Gregorc Associates.

Idaho State Department of Education. (1999). *A guide for starting and improving gifted and talented high school programs*. Retrieved October 30, 2004 from, http://www.sde.state.id.us/cdpubs/GTmanual.pdf

International Telementoring Program (ITP). (n.d.). Retrieved March 15, 2003, from www.telementor.org

Jekielek, S. M., Moore, K. A., Hair, E. C., & Scarupa, H. J. (2002). *Mentoring: A promising strategy for youth development*. Retrieved November 20, 2004, from http://www.childtrends.org/files/MentoringBrief2002.pdf

Jucovy, L. (2002). *Same-race and cross-race matching* (Technical Assistance Packet #7). Retrieved March 20, 2003, from Northwest Regional Educational Laboratory's Web Site: www.nwrel.org/mentoring

Kaufmann, F. (2003, Winter). Mentorships for gifted students: What parents and teachers need to know. *PAGE Update*, pp. 1, 5, 11.

Kettle, K. E., Renzulli, J. S., & Rizza, M. G. (1998). My way: An expression style inventory. *Gifted Child Quarterly, 42*, 48–61.

Lashaway-Bokina, N. (1996). *Gifted but gone: High ability, Mexican-American, female dropouts*. Unpublished doctoral dissertation, University of Connecticut, Storrs.

Letting Education Achieve Dreams (L.E.A.D.). (n.d.). *Mentoring.* Retrieved March 30, 2003, from http://www.uhv.edu/lead/mentoring.htm

Lupkowski, A. E., Assouline, S. G., & Stanley, J. C. (1990). Applying a mentor model for young mathematically talented students. *Gifted Child Today, 13*(2), 15–19.

McGreevy, A. (1990). Darwin and teacher: An analysis of the mentorship between Charles Darwin and professor John Henslow. *Gifted Child Quarterly, 34*, 5–9.

Milam, C. P. (2001). Extending learning through mentorships. In F. A. Karnes & S. M. Bean (Eds.), *Methods and materials for teaching the gifted* (pp. 523–558). Waco, TX: Prufrock Press.

Minority Engineering and Computer Science Program (n.d.). Retrieved April 1, 2003, from http://mecsp.cecs.ucf.edu/mentor.html

Nash, D. (2001, December). Enter the mentor. *Parenting for High Potential*, pp. 18–21.

Nash, D., & Treffinger, D. (1993). *The mentor kit: A step-by-step guide to creating an effective mentor program in your school.* Waco, TX: Prufrock Press.

National Mentoring Center. (n.d.). *Mentor recruitment postcard available for local programs.* Retrieved March 26, 2003, from http://www.nwrel.org/mentoring/

National Mentoring Partnerships. (n.d.). Retrieved March 23, 2003, from http://www.mentoring.org

Nebraska Department of Education. (1998). *Nebraska work based learning manual: Mentorships* . Retrieved February 22, 2005, from http://www.nde.state.ne.us/TECHPREP/WBL/WBL%20Manual.htm

Pennsylvania State University. (1999–2002). *The mentor: An academic advising journal.* Retrieved November 27, 2004, from http://www.psu.edu/dus/mentor/homer.htm

Purcell, J. H., Renzulli, J. S., McCoach, D. B., & Spottiswoode, H. (2001, December). The magic of mentorships. *Parenting for High Potential*, 22–26.

Reilly, J. (1992). When does a student really need a professional mentor? *Gifted Child Today, 15*(3), 2–8.

Renzulli, J. S. (1977). *The enrichment triad model: A guide for developing defensible programs for the gifted and talented.* Mansfield Center, CT: Creative Learning Press.

Renzulli, J. S., & Reis, S. M. (1985). *The Schoolwide Enrichment Model: A comprehensive plan for educational excellence.* Mansfield Center, CT: Creative Learning Press.

Renzulli, J. S., Rizza, M. G., & Smith L. H. (2002). *Learning styles inventory (Version III): A measure of student preferences for instructional techniques.* Mansfield Center, CT: Creative Learning Press.

Rimm, S. (2001, December). Parents as role models and mentors. *Parenting for High Potential,* 14–15, 27.

Rimm, S. (2003). *See Jane win for girls: A smart girl's guide to success.* Minneapolis, MN: Free Spirit.

Robb, E R. (1997). *The telementoring revolution: Three case studies.* Retrieved May 21, 2003, from http://www.ctcnet.org/telemcnt.html

Roberts, J., & Inman, T. (2001, December). Mentoring and your child: Developing a successful relationship. *Parenting for High Potential,* 8–10.

Shaughnessy, M. F., & Neely, R. (1991). Mentoring gifted children and prodigies: Personological concerns. *Gifted Education International, 7,* 129–132.

Siegle, D. (2001, December). "One size fits all" doesn't work when selecting a mentor. *Parenting for High Potential,* 7, 11.

Siegle, D., & McCoach, D. B. (2005). Extending learning through mentorships. In F. A. Karnes & S. M. Bean (Eds.), *Methods and materials for teaching the gifted* (2nd ed., pp. 473–518). Waco, TX: Prufrock Press.

Silverman, L. K. (2000). Career counseling. In L. K. Silverman (Ed.), *Counseling the gifted and talented.* (pp. 215–238). Denver, CO: Love.

Sternberg, R. J. (1994). Allowing for thinking styles. *Educational Leadership, 52*(3), 36–40.

Tomlinson, C. A. (2001, December). President's column. *Parenting for High Potential*, 5, 27.

Torrance, E. P. (1984). *Mentor relationships: How they aid creative achievement, endure, change, and die.* Buffalo, NY: Bearly Limited.

VanTassel-Baska, J. (2000). Academic counseling for the gifted. In L. K. Silverman (Ed.), *Counseling the gifted and talented.* (pp. 201–214). Denver, CO: Love.

YWCA at U.C. Berkeley. (n.d.). *Youth Mentor Program: Program descriptions.* Retrieved March 23, 2003, from http://www.ywca-berkeley.org/mentor.html

About the Author

Del Siegle serves on the executive board of the National Association for Gifted Children and The Association for the Gifted. Del is an associate professor in gifted and talented education at the University of Connecticut where he coordinates the Three Summers master's degree and online graduate classes program. His research interests include student motivation, teacher biases in identifying gifted students, and teaching with technology.

Printed in the United States
by Baker & Taylor Publisher Services